A South Lakeland

Nautical Dynasty

A South Lakeland
Nautical Dynasty

Captain Joseph Fayrer
of
Milnthorpe

Leonard Smith

LENSDEN PUBLISHING

Lensden Publishing
© Leonard Smith
Published 2012

ISBN 978-0-9551992-8-8

Front Cover: *Wreck of SS President,* Andreas Achenbach.
Back Cover Top to Bottom: *SS President,* 1840, Samuel
Walters; Sir Joseph Fayrer, 1st Baronet; Jamaica Postage
Stamp with West Indian Steam Packet Company ship,
RMS Thames; a Liverpool Slave Ship.

Printed by MTP Media, Beezon Fields, Kendal, Cumbria, LA9 6BL

Contents

Illustrations

Preface and Acknowledgments

The events described in this book took place in the late-Eighteenth and early to mid-Nineteenth centuries, after the Creek of Milnthorpe had begun to give up its trade to the larger ports of Lancaster and Liverpool

The movement away from Milnthorpe, which for three hundred years had served as Kendal's minor seaport, was partly a result of the increased dimensions of vessels, which could no longer navigate the restricted waters of the River Kent Estuary, and partly because Lancaster and Liverpool had developed as the principal ports for the Slave Trade and the privateering, which took place during the Revolutionary wars with France and America.

Milnthorpe nonetheless continued to handle imports and exports for Kendal, though tonnage was greatly reduced, and more so after the construction of the Kendal to Lancaster Canal, when seaborne cargoes could be loaded and discharged at a newly built quay at Hest Bank, and taken by narrow boat to and from the heart of Kendal. But the port's heyday was over and the death knell for its commercial traffic was finally struck by the coming of the railways and the building of the Kent Estuary viaduct in 1857.

With the decline, the port's mariners were forced to seek employment further afield. Where once they might have sailed directly from Sandside below Haverbrack Common to the American colonies, and later to the Baltic States until circa 1760, they now embarked at Lancaster or Liverpool. The Westmorland seaboard nonetheless remained their home, where their families continued to reside, and where they returned between voyages.

The principal maritime family connected with the small coastal town, Westmorland's only port, were the Fayrers, pronounced 'Fairer', whose doyen Captain Joseph Fayrer built a small mansion, Harmony Hill, later known as Harmony Hall, the town's largest house after Dallam Tower.

Unless the genealogy can be traced further back, it must for the present be assumed that Joseph Fayrer of Harmony Hill was the earliest of the family's mariners, and the first of a distinguished dynasty of seafarers who began their careers under his influence.

Captain Joseph Fayrer's life was traced briefly in my book *Kendal's Port: A Maritime History of the Creek of Milnthorpe*. Further research and new sources now make it possible to explain more of his exploits and to bring to light the equally interesting achievements of his son Commander Robert John Fayrer RN, and his grandson Sir Joseph Fayrer Bt FRS, who was initially a mariner and then a Naval surgeon, but later served in the Indian Medical Service and became a pioneer of Tropical Medicine.

The book will also relate the heroic tragedy of another of Captain Fayrer's sons, Midshipman Edward Birbeck Fayrer RN, who died in 1811, aboard the ill-fated *HMS Defence,* in a Christmas gale at the mouth of the Baltic Sea.

Most distinguished of all was Captain Fayrer's grandson and namesake, Joseph Fayrer, the first baronet, and if he receives least attention here, it is only because his achievements have already been more than adequately chronicled in his autobiography *Recollections of My Life*.

Just as the details of the Creek of Milnthorpe needed to

be recovered and recorded in *Kendal's Port*, now the careers and exploits of some of its leading mariners will be added to the largely forgotten record of maritime traditions surrounding the River Kent estuary, which today forms part of the Arnside and Silverdale Area of Outstanding Natural Beauty.

The research has been almost entirely a personal quest, but I am grateful for the correspondence I have had with Sir John Fayrer of Edinburgh, the present baronet, and conversations with Sir James Cropper, the Lord Lieutenant of Cumbria, whose Liverpool forebears, Cropper, Benson and Rathbone, owned the *Bengal*, the second ship to reach India after the ending of the East India Company's monopoly. Sir John has also kindly assisted with the proof-reading. Roger Bingham kindly identified Haverbrack Cottage for me. Peter Winterbottom, Secretary of the Society for Nautical Research, read the near final draft and kindly gave advice. Once again, Joan my wife has assisted with pre-press details.

A brief explanation of nautical ranks may be helpful. Captain Joseph Fayrer's title is the courtesy one afforded to masters of ships in the merchant service. His son, Robert John Fayrer is variously described as Lieutenant Fayrer RN, which, after service as a Midshipman, was his rank throughout his naval career until he retired as Commander in 1848; or as Captain Fayrer when in command of merchant ships, and sometimes even as Captain Fayrer RN, though in fact he never held the rank of Captain in the Royal Navy.

For the account of the Parliamentary Enquiry into the Slave Trade in Chapter 1, the original has been edited slightly for better understanding, but I have followed the official record by omitting quotation marks for the questions put to, and answered by Captain Fayrer.

Attempts have been made to secure permission for the publication of images where it is uncertain whether they are in the public domain, and I apologise for any failure to make acknowledgments that are due.

The Rev Sue Wilson, vicar of Heversham kindly gave permission to photograph the Fayrer memorial in St Peter's Church. The picture of the awkwardly placed and much faded tablet was taken by my son-in-law, Colin Reynolds.

Finally, perhaps it should be said that Haverbrack, where Commander Robert John Fayrer resided, is less significant today than in 1562, when it was specified for the collection of Custom duty for vessels casting anchor on the soil of Haverbrack common or Milnthorpe haven. The small hamlet, situated 1 mile SE of Sandside, is now approached from Beetham, or by the road passing in front of Dallam Tower.

Leonard Smith
Arnside, 2012

1

Captain Joseph Fayrer

Master Mariner
Slave Ship Captain and Privateer
Founder of a Nautical Dynasty

Family Origins

It is alleged that Joseph Fayrer was baptised on 17 July 1743, though the date and place of his birth and baptism has not been established, nor whether they were in the vicinity of Milnthorpe, where he was to settle. His will suggests he had a brother Edward and a sister Mary. He married Bridget, daughter of John Dickinson, on 7 April 1777.[1] His death occured in Africa on 11 January 1801, aged 57 years.[2]

Virtually nothing is known of his education. Possibly it could have been at Heversham Grammar School.[3]

It may be surmised however that he first went to sea as an apprentice in a Lancaster vessel, and possibly in a foreign-going ship sailing from the Creek of Milnthorpe.[4]

The admission of his son Robert John as a Freeman of the City of Lancaster in 1818 indicates that Joseph Fayrer must have been a Freeman before him. For unless that were so, it would have been necessary for his son to have completed indentures in the city, which was impossible, as he had served as a Midshipman in the Royal Navy from the age of fifteen years.[5]

Captain Fayrer's indentures, possibly of seven years duration, which was the usual term for eligibility as a Freeman, were probably completed sometime circa 1764, with his earliest voyages being from Milnthorpe, where the brigs *Fortune* and *Content* were still trading to the Baltic as late at 1759.

As a ship's officer he was first engaged in the trade to Africa in either 1770 or 1771, when he made two voyages as Mate before sailing for the first time as Master. There is little information about this period, but it is recorded that he was in command of the *Will* at Montego Bay on 21 December 1776, with a cargo of 288 Gold Coast slaves for the Hibbert, Bernard & Montague plantations. Shortly afterwards, this first period of Slave trading was interrupted by the War of Independence and the hostilities with America and France that took place between 1776 and 1783, when for several voyages Fayrer commanded privateer ships sailing from Liverpool under letters of marque.[6]

Captain Fayrer's marriage to Bridget Dickinson, the daughter of a Lancashire gentleman, at Kendal on 7 April 1777, produced ten children: Jenny, baptised 3 Oct. 1778; Maria, born 2 April 1784; Joseph, born 21 January 1786, died 10 May 1838; Robert John, born 11 March 1788, died 20 April 1869; Sally, born 7 May 1789; Edward Birbeck, born 9 May 1791, died 23 December 1811; Hannah, born 15 August 1792; Nancy, born 26 November 1794; Jane, born 20 August 1797, who married Nicholas Phillips RN; and one other daughter, born sometime before 1789.[7]

The Rev Joseph Fayrer married Sarah, the daughter of George Clay and became vicar of St Teath, Cornwall, in 1826; Hannah married the Rev Joseph Coates, vicar of Huddersfield, on 5 January 1815, and Nancy married the Rev John Kirkby MA of Underbarrow, Westmorland, Chaplain of *HMS Windsor Castle,* at Stonehouse, Devon, in 1825. A family memorial is sited in Heversham Church.

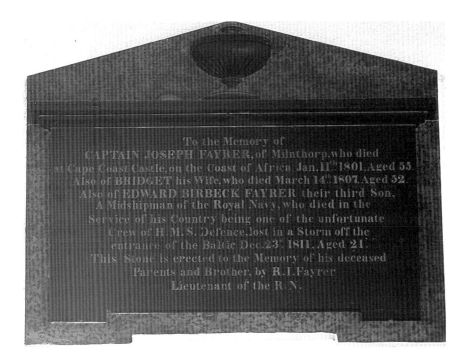

Fayrer Memorial, Heversham Church, Inscription below

To the Memory of Captain Joseph Fayrer of Milnthorpe, who died at Cape Coast Castle, on the coast of Africa Jan. 11th 1801, aged 55. Also of Bridget his Wife, who died March 14th 1807, Aged 52. Also of Edward Birbeck Fayrer their third Son, a Midshipman of the Royal Navy, who died in the Service of his Country being one of the unfortunate Crew of H.M.S. Defence lost in a Storm off the entrance of the Baltic Dec. 23rd 1811, Aged 21. This stone is erected to the Memory of his deceased Parents and Brother by R. I. Fayrer. Lieutenant of the R.N.

Slave Captain and Privateer

Captain Joseph Fayrer was first regularly employed as Mate and then as Master by Thomas Rumbold, one the principal Liverpool investors in the Slave Trade, and later by Messrs Earle and Sons. Details of some of his voyages in these employments were reported briefly in the newspapers of the period:

Adams's Weekly Courant (Chester, England) recorded that on Tuesday 16 February 1779, the *Rumbold* of Liverpool (Captain Fayrer), 250 tons, 20 guns and 57 men, took at the Isles de Los, the *Ulysses*, a French Guineaman, with 302 Slaves, and about two tons of Ivory.[8]

Two months later on 20 May 1779 the *General Evening Post* (London) told how, according to news received from St Jago de la Vega, Jamaica, the ship *Rumbold* (Captain Fayrer) had arrived at Kingston from Africa. Fitted out from Liverpool, on her arrival she had found a French Guineaman, fully slaved, and ready for sailing, which she boarded, took out the slaves, etc, and then scuttled her; the cargo consisted of 500 healthy slaves.[9]

The Will of Liverpool (on the left) engaging with a French Privateer

The *St James's Chronicle* (London) of 9 June 1781 listed Captain Fayrer as being in command of the *Harlequin,* a privateer. In a letter of 12 May 1781 to his owners, Earle and Sons of Liverpool, Fayrer had reported that he had two ships, the *Cervo* and the *Flore* in sight, bearing S.E., and that he had taken a Swedish brig, and by stratagem discovered she was sent out to give advice to the East Indiamen. He then detained another brig from Ostend, upon the same errand, which he intended to send home as a prize in a few days time. He also mentions being in company with the *Caesar* of Bristol, at the time of her capturing a ship from Curacoa. The prize arrived at Bristol a month later.[10]

On 28 June 1787, *The Whitehall Evening Post* (London) reported that Captain Fayrer of the *Mosley Hill*, a Baker and Dawson ship, which had arrived in Liverpool from Havana, had on the 3 June spoken with the *Shelbourne* (Captain Penny) from London, bound to Halifax, Nova Scotia in latitude 44°9' N, longitude 50°. Later, on the 6 June, in latitude 48°N longitude 42°32'W, he had spoken with the *Europe* (Captain Formitor) bound from Poole to Newfoundland, and on 12 June, in latitude 47°51'N, longitude 22°25'W, with *The Brothers*, from London for Newfoundland. Off Cape Clear, on the 16 June, he fell in with the *Bacchus* (Captain Hamilton), sailing from Antigua to Bristol, and found all was well.

Atlantic Icebergs

Aboard the *Mosley Hill*, on the same voyage, at latitude 45° N, longitude 46°59' W, Captain Fayrer was surprised to hear the helmsman calling out, 'Land!', when on coming on deck he perceived to his utter astonishment that the vessel was, as he supposed, within 200 yards of a tremendous rock, or island of ice, which appeared to be three times as high as the ship's top-gallant masthead, the circumference being as much as the ground on which the town of Liverpool stands. It was grounded in 35 fathoms and had the most rude, horrid, and terrifying appearance; it seeming to overhang the vessel, threatening to overwhelm her. The terror was considerably heightened by huge fragments loosening from the top, which falling down, and striking against its craggy sides raised such a smoke as ascended in columns magnificently grand and awful.[11]

The next morning the *Mosley Hill* fell in with another island of ice, but not of such great magnitude, it being not more than one-third its size. Its appearance was far different, the top and the sides being formed into beautiful plains and slopes, and the sun-beams playing on it gave it the appearance of polished silver; and being discovered at such a distance as to create no suspicions of danger, was viewed with great pleasure by the ship's company.[12]

On 22 October 1789, the *English Chronicle* (London) was reporting that Captain Briscoe of the ship *King's People* had arrived at Liverpool from Jamaica, with information that he had passed Havana earlier that month, with the *Mosley Hill* lying there, and that Captain Fayrer had come aboard in his hoy and said he expected to sail for Liverpool within a fortnight.[13]

Africa

After the preliminary peace agreement with the American colonies in 1782, and with France and Spain a year later, opportunities for privateering ceased and mariners, including Joseph Fayrer, returned to Slave trading.

As it became increasingly controversial, and against a background of pressure for its abolition, a Parliamentary Enquiry into the Slave Trade was held in 1792, at which Fayrer was one of a contingent of Liverpool merchants and captains, all members of the Africa Company, who made submissions in favour of the trade continuing.

The Enquiry provides the primary source of information

about Captain Fayrer's slaving voyages and the extent of his knowledge about the Trade. While there is no reason to doubt the factual accuracy of his submissions, it should nonetheless be borne in mind that they are biased in favour of the Trade being continued.

In his opening statement Fayrer said he had first become involved in the slave trade in either 1770 or 1771, and since then had made about eleven voyages, two as mate and the rest as master.

The following is a summary of the proceedings, the questions asked, and Captain Fayrer's replies:

Mr. Law, counsel for the several petitioners, requested permission to proceed upon the Petition of the Merchants, Traders, and Ship-owners, concerned in the African Slave Trade, and to proceed…to its Close, more particularly because a witness now attending was under the immediate necessity of returning to his ship, and proceeding upon his voyage. (This witness must have been Joseph Fayrer, who was called first, and his ship the *Golden Age*.) He was examined as follows:

When asked how long he had been employed in the African trade, Fayrer replied that it was about twenty years, and that part of that time, during the war, he was sometimes cruising, and then returned to the African trade again. Asked whether these voyages were uniformly to the same part of the Coast, or to different parts of it, Fayrer replied, to different parts of the coast, but mostly to the Gold Coast and to Whydah, in the first place; then three voyages to Bonny; then again to Whydah.

Asked if he was well acquainted with the manner of purchasing slaves, Fayrer replied, Certainly I am, having been on a number of voyages; and my conduct has always been approved of by my employers.

In reply to where he had taken the slaves on leaving the Coast, he answered, mostly to Jamaica, for the first part. And when asked if he were merely acquainted with the Coast, or with the interior as well, he replied, with both, the sea coasts I have traded with, and also some of the interior parts of Africa, particularly Whydah and the Kingdom of Dahomy, the inland part.

The Kingdom of Dahomy

Asked to specify when it was that he first went up into the interior part of the country, he replied, I think in the year 1783 or 1784; or in part of both those years I think I was there. And how far is Dahomy from the sea-coast? From the best calculation that I could make in the way we travelled, a hundred miles or upwards, I think.

Is Dahomy a state or kingdom, with a sovereign at the head of it? Most certainly it is; a very despotic kingdom too. What is the capital of it? Abomy is the capital of it; there are four palaces, Abomy, Aguina, Kclmina, and Adowy. Were you at all the places of which you have been speaking? Yes, at all of them. Were you there more than once, or once only? I was there several times.

Travel to the African Interior

The first time you went up, who accompanied you? The governor of the English fort at Whydah; Gug Wee is the name of the place where the English fort is. There is also a French fort and a Portuguese fort within pistol shot of each other.

In what way did you travel into the interior part of the

country? The only way of travelling is in hammocks suspended on a pole, unless we chose to walk, which would almost be impossible from the intense heat, and we mostly travel in the night, being much cooler, and better for the people who carry us. How long were you in going from the sea-coast to Abomy? About three days.

At what rate did you travel? I think at the rate of five miles an hour: they go exceedingly fast; they mostly ran with us; for when we got out to walk, the men that carried us were exceedingly impatient, and desired that we should get in, that they might get on the faster.

Did you go up in consequence of any invitation from the sovereign of the country, or of your own accord? It being about the time the king makes his customs, he wishes to see white people, and generally sends for the English governor, the Portuguese governor, and the French governor, and all the white people that will attend.

Was it upon an occasion of this sort that you went up? Partly by the king's desire, and in hopes of gaining some advantages in trade also.

Having spoken of the king making his customs, what is meant by that expression? The customs are to make human sacrifices, which are done in abundance in the most horrid manner.

In what way were you received upon your arrival at Abomy? When I came to the gates, there is a bridge that is thrown over an entrenchment into the place; our being there was announced to the king, and we were admitted; then we went on for some distance, about half a mile or a mile, till we came to a big tree, where we were desired to sit down. As the governor had been there before, they directed their civilities mostly to me, being a stranger; the governor went to the place allotted him to live in, and I was ordered to sit down under the tree. The first people that came to me were three or four eunuchs.

I really cannot speak to the number, at least I was told they were eunuchs; they asked me how I came there, whether I had met with any insult and how I was, and enquiries of that kind. After telling them I was very well another set of people came to me, which are called the king's half-heads, from their having one side of their heads shaved and the other quite bare; the ornaments they wore, at least they were pleased to call them ornaments, were human teeth strung in very great quantities over their shoulders, crossing at the breast.

After saying something to me in the same manner as the eunuchs, asking how I was, and so forth, they desired me to drink water and spirits brought by the eunuchs, by way of refreshment. After the half-heads left me, then came the captain of the soldiers, accompanied by a very large number of soldiers; much the same ceremony passed between him and me as from the others.

When this was over, they desired me to get into the hammock again; they carried me along to the king's door, where they danced and capered round me, and fired their muskets loaded with powder, and very much overcharged, I thought, a circumstance not very agreeable. On our way to the king's door, through the market-place, there were two human bodies hung by the heels; this shocked me very much indeed, and led me to inquire what was the cause of it; the reply the interpreter made to me was, they were there to take care of the market. Vultures were even fixed in the crutch of the poor creatures that were hung up, and were feeding upon their entrails, standing upon them as they were hanging; they had not been hung up there long before.

What was meant by taking care of the market? I apprehend what they meant by it was, that justice should be done, or that something of the kind would happen to those who did wrong; that is what I apprehended, but I never heard the reason.

The King of Dahomy

Were they malefactors? I cannot tell, I believe not.

Did you understand that this was a peculiar circumstance, or that it constantly or often happened? I was told from the natives that it was very frequent, that as one body fell to pieces another was put in its place.

Were they hung up alive, or after they were dead? After they were dead, I apprehend; their private parts being cut away, which I was told was that they should not give offence to the women in the market.

Besides what you have described, did you see anything else that struck you in passing along?

Not just at that time, not on my way to the king's door.

From the market-place I was carried directly to the king's door: when I came to the king's door, they ran with me very fast three times round a large tree, and at the king's door all the grandees were sitting to receive me; after going the third time round, they got up from the skins, and other things that they were sitting on, and welcomed me to the country. That ceremony over, I was then carried to the place allotted me to live in, the rabble and soldiers still dancing and capering round me. When I came to the house I was to reside in, I met with the governor; I there gave the captain of the soldiers, the principal eunuchs, and the principal of the half-heads, each a flask of brandy, which I understood it was the custom to do; when they had got the flask of brandy, the rabble dispersed. During the same day I saw a vast number of human heads in different places near the king's house, and over great men's doors, which the birds of prey were feeding on.

Describe the place in which the king resides? His house is walled in with a mud wall about fifteen feet high; the distance, as near as I could compute it to be, was about two miles and three quarters, or three miles and a half; but it was that at least; on the top of the wall human heads were also stuck, I believe about nine or ten inches, or a foot, distant; I cannot say the distance, but they were very near.

Were these heads planted at equal, or at nearly equal distances all round the circumference of the wall? Nearly round it; besides these there were a great number on the thatch, and other places about the king's house and the king's door.

Have you seen heads upon the walls surrounding other houses, as well as that in which the king resides? No, not on any other houses, only the king's houses; there are other of the king's houses that have some.

In passing through the town, did you or did you not observe several piles of human heads? I saw very large piles, and a great number of them.

Human Sacrifices

In what manner, and owing to what cause did you understand the deaths of these several persons to have been? Those that were piled up in that manner, I was told by the natives, were such as had been sacrificed annually in memory of, and to serve their late king: they imagine that they are to serve their king after death.

Are you to be understood to say, that these were sacrifices made upon the occasion of the death of the late king? There is annually a sacrifice made to the late king; but I shall speak of that. The last time I was up at Whydah, I wrote to a friend of mine about this voyage in a letter, giving him an account of this country merely for amusement.

Did you understand from the natives that this was a common or an uncommon event? A very common event; annually.

Did you then understand that human sacrifices were annually performed? Certainly, I understood it from everybody that spoke of it.

Did anything further pass that is material to relate, during the first time you were up at this place? Very material: after I had been up a little while, after two or three days, I was called to the king's door, and went accordingly. After we went to the king's door, we were desired to sit under a thatched shed. The king being acquainted with our being there, desired us to come in; the English governor was with me when I went to see the king; when we came into the king he was attended by a few women, and his grandees were lying prostrate at his feet, kissing the ground, and throwing dirt over their heads, as a token of submission, as I suppose. The conversation we had was upon different trifling matters; asking me how I came into the country? How I liked it, and things of that sort; and we were then dismissed. He reminded us of a present that is generally given to him; which we told him we would prepare and bring the next time; in two or three days after that, we told him that the present was ready, and we would wait upon him whenever he chose.

Did he express any concern to you, that you had not arrived sooner, so as to be present at these human sacrifices? After the first compliments were over, that was the first thing he said, that he was very sorry that I was not there at the time he made his sacrifice or customs. I told him I was very happy it so happened; for it was very contrary to the customs of white men.

You said the soldiers wore teeth as ornaments; did they wear any other ornaments of a peculiar sort? The drums of the soldiers were decorated with human skulls and jawbones, which they told me were the human skulls and jawbones of generals who they had taken in war.

Procuring Slaves

Did any war happen in the country shortly after your return from Abomy to the fort upon the coast? There did, which was the cause of my staying a very long time; for we had no trade during the war at all. The war was between that king and one at Port Agray.

Was the effect of this war to delay your stay in the country? It was really the case; there was no other reason given why we had no trade but the war.

From your experience of this particular trade, are wars among the native powers beneficial or injurious to the trade in slaves? Wherever I have been, wherever a war took place, it was always detrimental to trade, and very materially so.

Did you find more difficulty in procuring slaves when there were wars than when there was peace? When there were wars, as I said before, there was very great difficulty in procuring slaves.

Does this observation apply to Whydah only, or to all those parts of the Coast with which you are acquainted? Yes, upon the Gold Coast and at Whydah. At other places there have never been any wars while I have been there, that I know of.

From your knowledge of this trade, can it be in the interest of the European trader to promote wars between the native powers? Far to the contrary, as far as my knowledge of the trade can lead me to judge.

Do you know what became of the prisoners made in the war of which you have spoken? In the war that happened at Whydah when I was there, we understood from the natives, and many who had been there, and whom I saw and conversed with, that they were mostly killed, and their heads ordered to be carried up to the king of Dahomy.

Have you, or have you not, in fact, seen heads carried up in baskets for this purpose? I have, in great numbers, on men's heads, two or three in a basket together, and I think in some four, which were very offensive indeed, though they were at a good distance from me.

Were you able, during this war, to complete your purchase

of slaves? Far to the contrary, I think I only bought seven slaves during the war, during five months.

Was this, to the best of your knowledge, owing to the war? I was so informed by the natives.

In the same period of time, what number would you have expected to have purchased in time of peace? I should have expected, in that time, to have purchased at least 500.

How did war prevent it? By reason that the trading men and all the great men were obliged to attend the war, instead of going to market for trade.

Second Inland Journey

Having already said that you were a second time at Abomy, I wish to ask you what happened upon the second occasion? It was a consequence of the badness of the trade that I was induced to take a second journey up to Dahomy; I was in hopes I would have had some influence with the king to have gone on with my trade.

At what time did you make this second journey? I cannot justly speak to the time; it might be about six or seven months after, or eight months, in all probability.

What happened upon that occasion? It was in the rainy season, and I travelled with very great difficulty; one part of the road which they called the Bust, is dreadful indeed, very bad to get through; and I saw some human bodies lying there, their burden had been too much for them, and they had lain down and died there from the inclemency of the weather. From the fatigue in going up, I had not been in Dahomy above three or four days before I was taken exceedingly ill, and obliged to be carried down again. Were you also afterwards there? I was, in 1790 or 1791.

Who were the persons that went up with you? The second in command at the English fort went up with me; but there was at the same time a French governor, an English governor, the Portuguese governor, and a French captain.

Was this the time of what you have called custom making? It was indeed; it was a custom making to the last king that died, which was about a year and a half before that time.

Did you see any persons being carried on their way to be sacrificed? Yes, a great number. State nearly about how many, as accurately as you can. I cannot speak exactly; I suppose I might have seen 150, I think more.

In what state were they at this time? They were carried on men's shoulders, gagged; and they danced with them round our house, in order to let us see them, though we desired that they would not do so.

From the number of heads which you yourself saw upon this occasion, how many do you conceive the number sacrificed to have been? A great number of sacrifices were made daily for about a month, while I was there; but the latter sacrifice had been very great indeed, what they call their Grand Custom-day; and from the best calculations that the gentlemen who were with me could make, there were at least 500 heads cut off. The dead bodies frequently were carried past the place where we lived, or trailed along with a string tied to one of the legs of the headless body. We remonstrated against their bringing them that way; and at last the king ordered them not to come that way any more.

Were these scenes of exultation or of depression to the persons concerned in them? They were dancing, singing, and laughing, as they went along with them. Did they sacrifice men only, or men and women indiscriminately? Both sexes, but mostly men; and I think more old men than young. Do you know what sort of persons they were who were sacrificed upon these occasions? I have reason to believe they were the Dahomianc, the king's subjects, because they make a kind of distinction between those taken in war, and those that are to be sacrificed for the king. Those sacrificed for the king are generally given by the principal head trader and head men, according to their con-sequence; they give a number each of them to be sacrificed, and those heads are what are piled up, but the heads taken in war are generally stuck up round the walls.

Do you know what becomes of the blood shed upon those occasions? I was told by the natives that a great part of it was taken to mix with mud, in order to build a temple in memory of the late king; a Fetish-house, as they call it.

From your knowledge of the country, and of the manners of this people, would the abolition of the Slave Trade lessen the number of human sacrifices? It is my opinion that the sacrifices would be far greater were it not for the trade.

State your reasons why? There would be no market for them; and what gives me reason to believe so is, that it is young people only that we bring most often, and I saw a great number of those that were sacrificed were old; indeed, I have heard the great men say, that there was usually a greater number killed than was then; that was nothing; and they seemed to laugh at me when I talked of it with concern.

Are you then convinced that the purchasing of slaves is often the saving of their lives? I have very great reason to believe that it is.

While you were in the interior part of the country, did you yourself purchase any slaves? Most undoubtedly I did; and the first parcel that I was called to look at was seventeen.

State what happened to these men? They were fine young people, but exceedingly thin; on inquiring the cause, they told me they had been a long time confined, and that it was for want of victuals; they themselves put their hand upon their bellies, and said, 'Master, buy me, and give me victuals enough, enough, and you will soon see me strong,' and stretched out their arms.

Are the slaves in general desirous to continue in the situation in which they are, or to be purchased by European captains? From the manner of the behaviour of those first seventeen, I should say they would much rather be bought; they desired it, and I bought them, or rather agreed for them; after which, having an opportunity the next day to send them down to the ship, and messengers with them, I went to Tamigan, who was the person that showed them to me; he is what they call prime minister, next to the king, and he calmly told me the king had killed them the night before.

Was it explained to you why the king had killed them the night before? They told me that his Fetish man had told the king that there was immediate occasion for a sacrifice, and that he would give me others instead of them.

Have any slaves ever applied to you to buy them as an act of saviour and mercy to themselves? I was called to purchase many during my stay there; I mostly found them exceedingly thin, and from the causes I before stated; as I was told, they very rarely get one meal a day while they are in the trunk, as they call it, which is the place they keep them in, which the slaves that were shown me always complained of, and very often said, 'White man, buy me.'

Having bought them, had you ever any conversation with them about leaving them in their own country, or in case of their being on board of your ship, about sending them back again?

Upon going on board my ship, seeing some of those very people that were before so very thin look fat, sleek, and very hearty, it of course led me to say something to them and in a joking way I have said to them, 'Well, now you have got fat and strong, will you go back to Dahomy?' They have said, 'No, you do me well;' which is as much as to say, you treat me well; 'You give me plenty to eat, plenty to drink; if you cut our heads off, it makes no matter.'

What language did they speak in?

Through an interpreter: in their country, they said, they were not only starved, but they cut off their heads.

Had you any reason to suppose that any of these were convicts, or people guilty of crimes?

I apprehend there must have been a good many of them of that description.

Do you conceive that there were others sold who were guilty of no crime whatever?

I believe, from the caprice of their masters, sometimes for imaginary assaults, they are sent off from the country; I believe that may be the case very often.

Did you, during the long course of your continuance in the African trade, ever know an instance of a slave being purchased, who had been, sentenced to death in the way of this human sacrifice, whose life had been saved by his being bought? It is my opinion that a great many are; it is slavery with those, or death: to be sold, seems only a milder way of punishment than, death.

Were you ever eye-witness to any man's life being saved, that is, who was condemned to death by the custom of that country, and who was saved by being purchased for a slave?

I cannot say that I have been present at any time when any one person was saved.

Have you in your different conversations with the slaves when on board your ship, understood from them, that their lives had been saved by their being sold to Europeans?

I have been told by themselves, that they have been saved, that they were glad they were got there, for 'had I not come here my head would have been cut off;' that has been very frequently said.

When slaves have been in general brought on board of the ship, have they expressed satisfaction or dissatisfaction at their being brought into that situation?

Some, out of the interior parts of the country, may show a little fear at seeing a number of White men together ; but in a very little time they are reconciled, and seem very much contented indeed.

Have you ever had occasion to converse with the kings or with the chief people in these African States where slaves are procured, relative to any idea that had been started in this country concerning any restraint to be proposed on this trade? The last voyage I was there, having spoken of the Abolition of the Trade, I have sometimes, said to the great men, that it was thought it would be the case.

What was the answer that they made upon that? They generally said, white men were fools; they knew very well what to do with them if they did not buy them.

Did you ever understand from any of the people, from the black traders, that they had any eastern channel of conveying slaves out of Africa, as well as the western channel, with which we are so well acquainted? I have never understood any way that slaves went but by shipping.

Question repeated. I do not understand the question.

You being of course a seaman, having been many voyages to that country, must be aware that the eastern coast of Africa is bounded by the water as well as the western; do you therefore know, that the Slave Trade is carried on, upon the eastern coast of Africa, as well as upon the western, from whence all the European nations have hitherto supplied their West-India islands with slaves? All the slaves that I know of are conveyed from any port of Africa that I have been at, in shipping.

The black traders come, by their own accounts, very great distances from the interior part of the country; have these black traders ever informed you that people on the eastern side of the African coast had bargained with them for slaves, as they do upon the western coast? Do you know anything of the eastern coast of Africa? I know nothing of the eastern coast.

You know upon the map where it lies: the Red Sea and Babelmandel; do you know anything of them? I know there are those places.

Did any of the traders converse with you about the eastern coast, and the trade there? I cannot charge my memory that any of them have.

Respecting these human sacrifices, are they the effect of religious superstition, or of despotic and arbitrary power? Partly both.

Has the king of the country you have been speaking of a

very large standing army? The whole country is his army whenever he pleases.

But has the king what we call a standing army, independent of the citizens at large? Always.

To what amount? It is impossible for me to speak to the amount, but it is very considerable indeed.

Who got the better in that war that you have mentioned? The king of Dahomy.

During the course of your acquaintance with the African coast, have you found greater difficulty in purchasing females than in purchasing males? In some parts of the coast more so than in others.

But in general did you find more ease in purchasing male slaves than in purchasing females? On the Gold Coast we find a greater difficulty in purchasing females; on the other parts we just take them as they come.

The witness (Captain Fayrer) was directed to withdraw. The Counsel were directed to withdraw.[14]

Dalzel's History of Dahomy

Joseph Fayrer's pre-eminent knowledge of the Trade was the reason why, when Archibald Dalzel, the Governor of the Gold Coast, published his *History of Dahomy*, in 1793, he was asked to write the Preface, in which he argued for the continuance of the Trade, maintaining that slaves were better off being transported than suffering the sacrifices at home. Dalzel himself only wrote the introduction and conclusion, while the text was largely the work of Robert Norris and Lionel Abson, two traders who had been engaged on the spot in the the African Company's service.[15]

The West India Merchant Network

Fayrer's role as the key witness for the Liverpool African Company's pro-Slave Trade stance at the Parliamentary Enquiry of 1792 also suggests the important position he occupied within the Trade, and his extensive knowledge of it in both Africa and Jamaica. Not only was he a successful slave ship master, but he had also become an investor in the Trade himself, and unlike those who only invested, his voyages acquainted him with the network of merchants and factors resident in the West Indies.

As Sheryllynne and John Haggerty have observed in their paper 'Visual Analytics of an Eighteenth-Century Business Network', a number of ships' captains, such as Thomas Rives, William Horsley, and Joseph Fayrer, were equally important as investors. They had conducted more than one voyage and would have current knowledge of the Trade. They also had direct contact with Plantation owners in Jamaica and had built up relationships with them. Ships' captains were therefore important not only in terms of their skills and knowledge of the Trade itself, but often as the only people to have regular contact with the factors in the West Indies. The Haggertys' paper describes this function as one of 'in betweeness.'[16]

Joseph Fayrer, they say, had relatively good 'betweeness centrality' within the network of factors, being far more important than some principal investors. He was incredibly well connected because he worked for Thomas Rumbold, one of the early principal investors, but more importantly, because of his links with the Heywood subnet, which was reinforced when he invested in this network himself.[17]

The Golden Age

Captain Fayrer acquired his own ship, the *Golden Age*, 377 tons burden, around 1788. She was probably bought with the Prize money from vessels he had captured as a privateer during the hostilities with France and America. It may have been a case of owning her outright, or more likely holding the majority of shares, which was always a safeguard against loss. He continued to command the vessel until she was sold, either in preparation for his semi-retirement from seafaring, or because he could foresee a successful outcome to the campaign for the Abolition of the Slave Trade. Some details of the ship's voyages may be gleaned from the Shipping Intelligence that was a common feature of many Eighteenth-century newspapers.

For example, *Woodfall's Register* (London) reported on 3 August 1793 that Captain Fayrer of the *Golden Age*, which left Grenada only five days ago, had mentioned how Admiral Gardner, with nine ships of the line, was then before Martinico.[18]

In London, the *Evening Mail* of 14 October 1793 reported information it had received from Cork, that the ship *Golden Age*, Captain Fayrer, belonging to Liverpool, had sailed from Jamaica five days after the fleet. Carrying several opulent merchants and planters as passengers from Jamaica, she had joined the fleet for some days afterwards, keeping company with the convoy before parting, only to be captured by the *Sans Culottes*, a privateer of 36 guns belonging to Bordeaux, which also took a vessel called the *Courier*, whose cargo of ivory they took out. They ransomed the vessel for £300. On arrival at Liverpool, for want of provisions and water the passengers were landed at Dingle.[19]

Harmony Hall, Milnthorpe

Harmony Hall

The proceeds of Privateering and the Slave Trade not only enabled Captain Fayrer to purchase his own ship, the *Golden Age*, but also to erect a small mansion for himself at the head of the market place in Milnthorpe. Harmony Hall, as the building is now named, is a relatively late affectation, for as late as 1819, when it was sold after the protracted settlement of Joseph Fayrer's will, it was still known and advertised as Harmony Hill. The house is Milnthorpe's finest after Dallam Tower. Nicholas Pevsner described it as being of the early-Nineteenth century, but Roger Bingham's claim that it belongs to the 1780s, on the grounds of its similarity to the work of the Carrs of York, accords more precisely with the peak of Fayrer's financial success, when he desired a home to reflect his status, suitably surmounted by a rooftop platform to provide a view over the Creek of Milnthorpe.[20]

The focus of Fayrer's work was now increasingly in Liverpool, where Lancaster slave ships were being transferred, making it surprising that he should have had any strong reasons for continuing to reside at Milnthorpe.

It had however been his home for most of his adult life, and the place where all his children were born. It may also be inferred from a statement by his son, Commander Robert J Fayrer RN, that in spite of lack of precise knowledge of his roots, he was definitely of Westmorland stock.[21]

There are no records of how Captain Fayrer travelled between Harmony Hill and Liverpool, but it is highly probable that he would have found the sea route more convenient than using the Kendal to Liverpool stagecoach.[22]

Seaborne traffic between Milnthorpe and Liverpool was an important feature of the Slave Trading enterprise. Locally manufactured gunpowder was shipped from the Creek of Milnthorpe to the magazines at Liverpool before being forwarded to Africa to be exchanged for slaves, who were taken on the infamous Middle Passage for sale in the West Indies.

At Liverpool, Fayrer acted as agent for the Low Wood Gunpowder Company, informing fellow directors of the amounts of powder required for shipment to Africa, and arranging for the purchase of quantities of saltpetre to be shipped to Milnthorpe for its manufacture. Moreover, when Harmony Hill was built, Fayrer was nearing the end of his own seafaring, and increasingly paying attention to his role as an agent, based on his long experience of Africa and the West Indies. Being in Liverpool he was conveniently placed to know the state of the markets.

Agent for Low Wood Gunpowder Works

The Lowood Gunpowder Company, which originated at Low Wood, near Ulverston, had been founded by Joseph Fayrer along with Daye Barker (the senior partner), James King, and Christopher Wilson, junior, of Kendal. The licence to manaufacture gunpowder at Low Wood was obtained at Lancaster Quarter Sessions on 2 October 1798.

The company also owned another site on the River Weaver at Acton, Cheshire, where there were nitre beds, from which Fayrer sourced saltpetre for shipment down the River Weaver to Liverpool, for its onward passage to the small ports around Morcambe Bay, including Milnthorpe.[23]

Liverpool Ships fitted-out for the Slave Trade

The state of the Slave Trade would also have been of general interest to Gunpowder manufacturers, as Africa was their principal market until the Trade was abolished. From his second home at Liverpool, Fayrer was ideally placed to provide the information they required. In a letter of 6 March 1800 he wrote to Christopher Wilson of Kendal concerning arrangements for the transport of gunpowder to Africa, expressing the hope that Parliament would not proceed to the Abolition of the Trade.[24]

On 3 October 1800, he followed this with a list of ships, their captains and the numbers of slaves they shipped from various African ports, including the *Annabella* and the *Bud*, which sailed from the Gold Coast carrying 225 and 190 slaves, respectively, with Fayrer himself in command.[25]

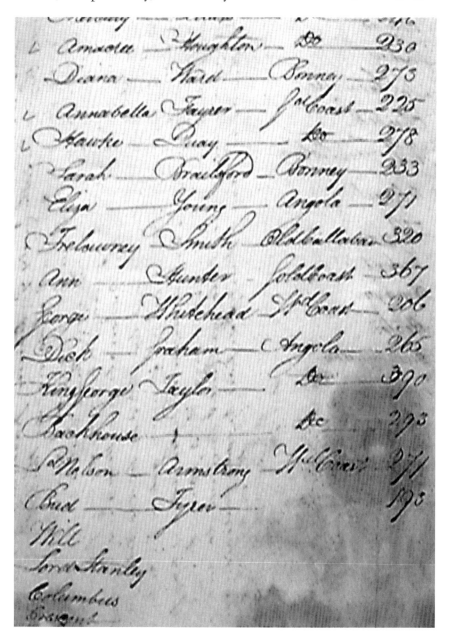

List of Slave Ships, Masters and Number of Slaves Transported

Captain Fayrer's Death at Cape Coast Castle

Captain Fayrer died at Cape Coast Castle in Africa on 11 January 1801. It has been said that he was visiting a son who was an agent on the Gold Coast, but this seems unlikely, as his son Joseph was vicar of St Teath, Cornwall, and Robert John Fayrer and Edward Birbeck Fayrer, were both serving in the Navy.[26]

To his wife Bridget, he left a life interest in Woodburn Cottage, Milnthorpe, but probate was not finally granted until there had been an Act of Parliament in 1819, when it was ruled that 'certain Estates devised by his Will, and now held in undivided Shares, in a Trustee, were to be sold; and investing the Purchase Monies of the Shares of such of the Parties interested as are Infants in the Purchase of other Estates to be conveyed to them in lieu of the Shares sold.' 59 Geo. 3. c.46. The principal beneficiaries were John Fayrer Coates and Bridget Coates, the children of his daughter Hannah.[27]

Cape Coast Castle

2

Commander Robert John Fayrer, RN

Naval Officer
East India Free Mariner
Pioneer of Steamship Navigation

Robert John Fayrer was the second son of Captain Joseph Fayrer and his wife Bridget, of Harmony Hill, Milnthorpe. He was born on 11 March 1788 and baptised at Heversham Church on 7 April. His elder brother, the Rev Joseph Fayrer, born 21 January 1786, became vicar of St Teath, Cornwall.[1]

Naval Career

Robert J Fayrer entered the Royal Navy on 11 November 1802 as a First Class Volunteer on board *HMS Caroline*, 36 guns (Captain Benjamin Page), stationed in the East Indies, where he served his qualifying period for appointment to the rank of Midshipman. From September 1803 he was with Captain (later Sir) Josiah Coghill, as Midshipman and Master's Mate in the sloop *HMS Rattlesnake,* where his companions in the midshipmen's berth were the Hon.William John Napier, later ninth Lord Napier of Merchistoun[2], and Frederick Marryat, who on retirement from the Navy as a Captain became the author of *Masterman Ready, Peter Simple* and *Mr Midshipman Easy*, all of which reflect the life Fayrer would have experienced early in his naval career.[3]

Frederick Marryat   The Hon. William John Napier

Whilst in *Rattlesnake*, Fayrer was in action with Malay proas (small ships); and, on his removal to *HMS Concorde*, he commanded the frigate's launch at the cutting out of the French brig *Vigilante*', 4 guns.

Joining next *HMS Imperieuse*, 38 guns (Captain Lord Cochrane), he served with great activity on the coasts of France and Spain, until he was compelled to invalid in February 1807, as a consequence of wounds, including a shattered arm, received when in the act of boarding an enemy's vessel in open day.[4] The incident is described by Florence Marryat in the *Life and Letters of Captain Frederick Marryat*, her father.

On Sunday, the 15th of November 1807, the *Imperieuse* having then sailed from Malta about ten days, and, with light and baffling winds, coasted down the shores of Sicily, we observed a large polacre ship (Mediterranean lateen rig) inshore. When we first saw her the wind was very light, and soon afterwards it fell calm. The warlike appearance of the vessel was too suspicious to allow her to pass unnoticed: it was evident that she was an armed vessel, and built for fast sailing, and the general opinion was that it was a Genoese privateer. The boats were hoisted out, and, under the command of Napier and Fayrer, sent away to examine her. As soon as they were within half a mile, the ship hoisted English colours. The sight of those colours, of course, checked the attack; the boats pulled slowly up towards her, and, when within hail, demanded what she was, for, if an English vessel, she could have no objection to be boarded by the boats of an English frigate. Now, as it afterwards was proved, the ship was a Maltese privateer of great celebrity, commanded by the well-known Pasquil Giliano, who had been very successful in his cruises, and, if report spoke truly, for the best of reasons, as he paid very little respect to any colours; in fact, he was a well-known pirate, and, when he returned to Malta, his hold was full of goods taken out of vessels, which he had burnt that he might not weaken his crew by sending them away; and in an admiralty court so notoriously corrupt as that of Malta, inquiries were easily hushed up. Although such was the fact, still, it had nothing to do with the present affair.

When the boats pulled up astern the captain of the polacre answered that he was a Maltese privateer, but that he would not allow them to come on board; for, although Napier had hailed him in English, and he could perceive the red jackets of the marines in the boats, Giliano had an idea, from the boats being fitted out with iron thole pins and grommets (for the oars), like the French, that they belonged to a ship of that nation. A short parley ensued, at the end of which the captain of the privateer pointed to his boarding nettings triced up, and told them that he was prepared, and if they attempted to board he should defend himself to the last. Napier replied that he must board, and Giliano leaped from the poop, telling him that he must take the consequences. The answer was a cheer, and a simultaneous dash of the boats to the vessel's sides.

A most desperate conflict ensued, perhaps the best contested and the most equally matched on record. In about ten minutes, the captain having fallen, a portion of the crew of the privateer gave way, the remainder fought until they were cut to pieces, and the vessel remained in our possession. And then, when the decks were strewed with the dying and the dead, was discovered the unfortunate mistake which had been committed. The privateer was a large vessel, pierced for fourteen guns and mounting ten, and the equality of the combatants, as well as the equality of the loss on both sides, was remarkable. On board of the vessel there had been fifty-two men; with boats, fifty-four. The privateer lost Giliano, her captain, and fifteen men; on our side we had fifteen men killed and wounded. Fayrer lost for ever the use of his right arm by a musket bullet, and Napier received a very painful wound, and had a very narrow escape, the bullet of Giliano's pistol grazing his left cheek and passing through his ear, slightly splintering a portion of the bone.

The *Imperieuse* returned to Malta with the privateer and the wounded men, and I never, at any time, saw Lord Cochrane so much dejected as he was for many days…[5]

Captain Lord Thomas Cochrane RN

Captain Lord Thomas Cochrane, later, from 1831, the 10th Earl of Dundonald, under whom Fayrer served in *HMS Imperieuse*, was one of the most remarkable Naval commanders of the Napoleonic Wars, simultaneously pursuing a political career as a radical Member of Parliament while still serving in the Navy.

In fiction, Thomas Cochrane was the model for C S Forrester's Horatio Hornblower, while Patrick O'Brian adopted him for his hero, Captain Jack Aubrey, in the Aubrey-Maturin series, the first volume being *Master and Commander,* which was later adapted for the cinema.

Captain Lord Thomas Cochrane

Cochrane stood for a seat in the House of Commons at the General Election in June 1806, on a ticket of parliamentary reform (a movement which would later bring about the

Reform Acts). He first contested the potwalloper borough of Honiton, Devon. It was exactly the kind of constituency he wished to see abolished, where votes were mostly sold to the highest bidder. Cochrane offered no bribes and consequenly lost the election. But he ran for Honiton again in October 1806 and won, later revealing how on that occasion he had paid ten guineas per voter.

At a more democratic election in May 1807, he contested the Westminster constituency, where he allied himself with the Radicals: William Cobbett, Sir Francis Burdett and Henry 'Orator' Hunt. His outspoken criticism of the conduct of the war and the corruption in the Navy made him powerful enemies in the government and at the Admiralty.[6]

Fayrer's Promotion to Lieutenant

Midshipman Robert John Fayrer was promoted to the rank of Lieutenant on 19 December 1808 while serving as a Supernumerary in the *Royal William* (Captain the Hon. Courtenay Boyle), the flag-ship at Spithead, where he must have prepared for the Lieutenants' examination. Afterwards, in February 1809, he was appointed, again as Lieutenant, to the *Nayaden* (Captain Frederick Cottrell), deployed off Greenland, and in the East and West Indies. On 1 February 1811 he transferred to the *Orpheus,* 36 guns (Captain Hugh Pigot). In September 1813 he was aboard the *Andromeda,* 22 guns (Captain Richard Arthur), stationed off the coasts of Spain and Portugal, and for his passage home from the Mediterranean on 4 July 1814 he sailed in the *Pompee,* 80 guns (Captain Sir James Athol Wood).[7]

Marriage at Beetham and Freeman of the City of Lancaster

In the more settled times that followed the ending of the

Napoleonic Wars, after the victory at Waterloo in 1815, Robert John Fayrer married Agnes Wilkinson of Kendal at Beetham Church on 12 August 1817.[8]

Two years later in 1819, he was admitted as a Freeman of the City of Lancaster, presumably taking advantage of the fact that his father had been a Freeman before him. With opportunities for his active service in the Navy now greatly reduced, he probably took this step to further his prospects of employment in connection with Lancaster merchants, several of whom also had shipping interests in Liverpool.

Half-Pay

Like so many other naval officers, Lieutenant Fayrer was on half-pay from 1814, plus a pension of £91. 5s per annum, for his wounds. But he was more fortunate than most. The ending of the war with France had virtually coincided with the termination, in 1813, of the East India Company's monopoly of trade with the Indian Sub-continent, opening up fresh opportunities for merchants in Liverpool, where his now deceased father, Captain Joseph Fayrer, had been extremely well connected with mercantile marine interests. On these foundations Fayrer was able to build a highly successful second career in the Merchant Marine.

East India Free Mariner

Benson, Cropper and Rathbone, the Liverpool merchants, lost no time in seizing the chance, and as early as 1816 they had arranged for the construction of the *Bengal*, 410 tons, especially for the Indian trade. Built at Greenock, on the Clyde, she sailed direct from Liverpool to Calcutta with Lieutenant Fayrer in command. She was the second ship to arrive there unrestricted by East India Company regulations.

After a further voyage in the *Bengal,* in 1821 Fayrer made two more voyages to India in command of another Benson and Cropper ship, the *Albion*, 505 tons. Later, after he had left her, the *Albion* was engaged in the Liverpool to New York Packet Service, for the Black Ball Line. She was wrecked off the coast of Ireland in 1822.[9]

The Bengal, 410 tons

Haverbrack Cottage, Milnthorpe, was still the home of the Fayrers at this time, and it was from there, in July 1821, while ashore, that Lieutenant Fayrer provided a festive tea party for the residents of Milnthorpe to celebrate the Coronation of King George IV, the former Prince Regent.[10]

The Cropper family, part owners of the *Bengal,* later gave up their shipping interests, moving from Liverpool to establish the paper manufacturing company at Burneside, near

Kendal. The Westmorland connections between the owners and master of the ship are however perhaps only a coincidence recognized with the passage of time.

For several more years Robert Fayrer continued to make voyages to the sub-Continent as a Free Mariner, but his ports of departure were now mainly on the south coast, particularly Portsmouth, which was more convenient for the embarkation of his influential passengers.

Landing Passengers at Madras

The tenancy of Haverbrack Cottage was relinquished in 1822. A new lease advertised in the *Lancaster Gazette* offered a genteel residence consisting of two parlours, four bed-chambers, two servants' rooms, and two kitchens, with other conveniences. The description is hardly one of a 'cottage', as now understood, and it seems probable that the property in question is what is today known as Haverbrack House.[11]

Voyages to India continued to be made from South Coast

ports until 1827, so perhaps the family divided their time between Portsmouth and Milnthorpe.

On 7 March 1825, *The Morning Post* reported from Portsmouth that the free-trader, *Madras*, Captain Fayrer, which drove on shore in the gale of 21 November last, had sailed with passengers for Madras, whilst on 23 January 1826, the *Caledonian Mercury* informed readers that Sir Edward Paget, the Commander in Chief for India, had booked his passage home in the *Madras* (Captain Fayrer), and was to sail about the middle of November direct.[12]

Fayrer's last ship for passages to India was the *Lady Flora*, 800 tons. The *Hampshire Telegraph and Sussex Chronicle* reported on 11 June 1827, that on Tuesday night the *Lady Flora* (Captain Fayrer) had arrived at St Helens, Portsmouth, from Calcutta, to land her passengers. She had left the Hoogly on the 11 February, and St Helena on the 28 April, carrying a valuable cargo of Indigo. After an outbound passage of only ten months and three days from Spithead, she had landed a heavy cargo of shot and ordnance stores at Calcutta, shipping her homeward cargo and embarking her passengers. She did not bring any political news…[13]

Bankruptcy

An unfortunate consequence of a voyage in the *Lady Flora* was that from 1831 Fayrer found himself embroiled in a court case, which led him to be declared bankrupt in the Court of Chancery in 1834. Like other officers, he was legitimately allowed to engage in some private trade. In this instance he had purchased wine at Maderia for sale in India, on behalf of Ullock and Co, wine merchants of London, and the plaintiffs maintained that he remained indebted to them for the proceeds of sales, some £1,500, while Fayrer argued that he had not received the money from India.[14] While the litigation was proceeding he resided at Ambleside.

Irish Steam Packet Company

When the case was concluded, Fayrer took up an appointment with the Irish Steam Packet Service, moving to Portpatrick to command *Spitfire*, built at Harwich in 1824. She was one of two steam packet paddle steamers carrying mail and passengers between Portpatrick and Donagahadee, the other being the *Fury*. Both ships were commanded by erstwhile naval officers, which was customary in the Post Office Packet services.

Spitfire was a mere 106 tons, and the *Fury*, also built at Harwich a year earlier, was of similar size. They were tiny by comparison with Fayrer's earlier sailing ships, but they provided experience for the significant transition he would shortly make from sail to steam for Transatlantic crossings.[15]

Steam Packet Ship 'Spitfire'

Intellectual and Scientific Interests

Robert J Fayrer was a man of broad interests extending well beyond his professional ones as a Naval Officer and Master Mariner. They included natural history and engineering. He was a member of the Royal Geographical Society and a Corresponding Member of the Zoological Society of London. He was also a donor of natural history specimens to several museums.[16]

While resident at Portpatrick he took an interest in local affairs on both sides of the North Channel, gifting several items of interest to the Belfast Museum, including a Madagascar broom, paper made in India from bamboo, and several specimens of mammals, and birds from Scotland.[17]

On one occasion, when the *Lady Flora* entered Portsmouth from Calcutta, it was reported that she carried two tigers, an ourang outang, and a wombat (the latter animal the first of its species ever in England), as presents to the Zoological Society. She also had on board a very fine leopard, destined for the same repository; it got loose however, and, as no means could be devised for securing it, it was necessary to resort to the alternative of shooting it.[18]

Later, in 1844, while on *HMS Tenedos* he presented two specimens of Snowy Owls to the Zoological Society.[19]

Steam Firefighting Equipment

The invention of a system for fire fighting at sea using steam was reported in the *Morning Chronicle* of 12 September 1838, when a correspondent wrote that on the previous Saturday, Lieutenant Robert John Fayrer RN, commanding the transatlantic steamship *Liverpool,* had the honour of an audience with HRH the Duke of Sussex, at Kensington

Palace, for the purpose of explaining the mode of applying his plan for extinguishing fire by steam on board steam ships, arising from the spontaneous combustion of coals or other causes. The plan, it was said, was considered by many of the most scientific engineers and other highly competent judges to be infallible; and His Royal Highness was pleased to express himself much gratified with the explanation given by Lieutenant Fayrer of his ingenious invention, and considered it entitled to the serious attention of all parties connected with steam navigation, particularly in large steamers performing long voyages. Lieutenant Fayrer's splendid ship the *Liverpool*, of 464 horse power, and upwards of 1,050 tons burden, intended for the American station, between Liverpool and New York, was fitted with his plan, which will no doubt inspire confidence in her passengers, the apparatus being so arranged as to convey the extinguishing power to all parts of the ship; thus triumphing over that most dreadful of all enemies - fire at sea - by the same power which is employed in propelling her to her destination. Lieutenant Fayrer's plan had been submitted to the Lords of Admiralty, and it was hoped would be generally adopted by the steamers in her Majesty's service.[20]

Safety Steering Wheel

To the Society of Arts, in 1850, Captain Fayrer read a paper and exhibited a model of his Safety Steering-wheel for preventing accidents that occur to helmsmen of large vessels, owing to their want of command over the wheel. The additional control was gained by the use of a friction band passing round the wheel, similar to those used in cranes, and connected with a pedal by which any amount of retarding pressure may be exerted by the helmsman. The invention was calculated to be also very efficient in preventing the wear and tear arising from the constant motion of the rudders of ships lying in tideways or harbours. With a Lt Robinson, a patent was secured and the invention was fitted to *HMS Niobe* and other ships between 1865-1876.[21]

Model of Lieut Fayrer's Safety Steering Wheel with foot operated Friction Band

The SS Liverpool

The 1830s saw the development of steamships for the transatlantic trade. The Transatlantic Steamship Company, a subsidiary of the Dublin Steamship Company, which operated the *Royal William*, was formed in 1837, and owned only one steamship, the *ss Liverpool*, which made seven transatlantic voyages before being sold to P&O. Built at the Humble & Milcrest yard in Liverpool, the 1150 ton vessel was the first two-funnelled steamer to cross the Atlantic. When P&O acquired her in 1840 she was renamed the *Great Liverpool*, and was wrecked in 1846 off Cape Finisterre.

As one of the most experienced steamship captains, Fayrer was given command of the *Liverpool*, for what turned out to be a not altogether successful experimental first voyage to Ireland in 1837, before he undertook the crossing from Liverpool to New York.

The *Liverpool* arrived at New York on 23 November, taking 16.5 days from Cork, in spite of very rough weather. Her return voyage was delayed until 6 December so she might carry the message that the US President, Martin van Buren, was to deliver at the opening of Congress.

SS Liverpool

On the evening before the termination of the homeward passage there was much conviviality and Mr Robert Gray composed *A Song: When we first Braved the Ocean Wave*, which he dedicated to Captain Fayrer and later published as sheet music for pianoforte.

The ship arrived in Liverpool on 22 December, to the

gratification of her passengers who addressed their testimonial to Captain Fayrer and presented him with an engraved gold snuff box.

To Captain Fayrer, RN
Steamship Liverpool, December 19, 1838

Dear Sir, Before the termination of our short and prosperous voyage, we cannot refrain from some expression of those sentiments of regard and esteem to which your uniform kindness and attention to our comforts have naturally given rise.

If any distrust in the qualities of the *Liverpool* were excited by her return to Cork upon her outward passage, her subsequent completion of the voyage to New York, against such weather as she encountered, must have dissipated that distrust. We have seen enough weather on this voyage to feel and know that all such apprehensions are thoroughly unfounded - that so long as she is under the able and skillful management of yourself and M T Shaw (to whose anxious attention to his duties, and courteous conduct to all on board, we are scarcely less indebted than to yourself), the safety and comfort of passengers by the *Liverpool* will be placed beyond doubt.

To your unvaried urbanity, politeness, and attention must be attributed the uninterrupted harmony which has reigned during our short and - though somewhat boisterous - very pleasant voyage; which together with your excellent table and good cheer, has reconciled us to a winter passage across the Atlantic.

To that voyage we shall ever look back with the kindliest feelings towards all connected with the *Liverpool,* and every sentiment of esteem and regard towards yourself, as some small token of which, we beg your acceptance of a gold snuff box, which Mr Ingram has undertaken shall be presented to you.

That you and your family may enjoy prosperity and health, with every happiness and comfort which you so well know how to impart to those who have the pleasure of being passengers under your command, is the anxious hope of,

Dear Sir, your sincere and faithful friends.
Signed (26 passengers)[22]

A Gold Snuff Box presented to Captain R J Fayrer of the SS Liverpool

Possibly it may have been the success of the voyage that led Fayrer to be granted honorary membership of the United States Navy Club in 1838, the first foreigner to be so admitted.[23]

The SS President

Lieutenant Fayrer's services were next sought by the British American Steam Navigation Company to command their new steamship *President,* fitted with lateral paddle wheels. After the *British Queen*, the company had ordered this second vessel, practically a sister ship, from Curling and Young. The new steamer was scheduled for launching on 7 December 1839, but the first attempt failed because the tide was not high enough. A second launch was not successful either, and she only took to the water on 9 December 1839. She was then towed down the River Thames from Limehouse Dock to Blackwall, where she was docked. Later the same month she sailed for Liverpool, where the two lateral balance engines manufactured by Fawcett and Preston were to be installed.

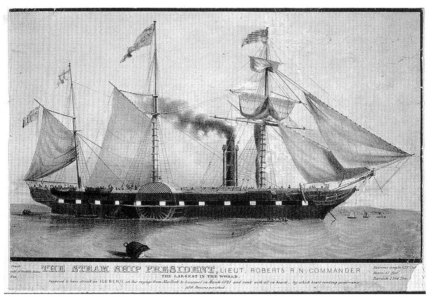

Lithograph of the SS President

On passage in the Channel the ship suffered considerable storm damage however, which coupled with ballast problems forced her to put into the Plymouth dockyard for repair work. Experts deemed her sailing properties to be unsound; she was said to be top heavy, and she rolled to a disquieting degree, even in relatively calm waters, a problem compounded because her engines were not yet fitted. After repairs, the *President* reached Liverpool without further problems. Her two engines had an output of only 540 h.p., which was too little for a ship of her size. She differed from other paddle steamers in having three decks instead of one.

This made her look bigger, even though she was somewhat shorter than the *British Queen*. In fact, she looked similar to a frigate, not least because she was adorned with painted ports. Built of oak, with pine planking and a continuous upper deck, she had three masts, two of which were abaft the funnel, and she was schooner rigged.

Another contemporary lithograph gave an impression of the interior furnishings. The dining room was about 12.5m wide and 26.5m long. On the left side, the ladies' lounge was visible; to the right there was a corridor leading to the two- and four-berth cabins, in which one hundred and ten passengers could be accommodated. Second class accommodation for forty-four passengers was forward of the engine room.

The stern was adorned with the British and American flags as well as a lion and an eagle. The figurehead was a portrait of George Washington. The cases of the paddle wheels were each decorated with a pentangular star. Before she went on her maiden voyage, the ship was open to the public on 30 July 1840. Admission tickets at a price of one shilling could be obtained from the office of the shipping company, and the proceeds were to be used for charitable purposes to be chosen by the mayor.

The *President* sailed from Liverpool on 1 August 1840 under the command of Capt R J Fayrer, lieutenant of the Royal Navy, with only a few passengers, as the *Great Western* and the *Acadia* were leaving for New York about the same time. She reached New York on 17 August, after 16 days, at an average speed of 8.4 knots. Compared with the *Great Western's* speed, this was not very satisfactory. Worse still, and more detrimental for the reputation of the shipping company, the *President* was overtaken on her maiden voyage by the steamer *Acadia* owned by the new competitor Samuel Cunard, in spite of having left Liverpool three days later. Cunard had succeeded in obtaining the mail contract on 4 May 1839, which was subsidised with £55,000 from the British Admiralty. Together with George Burns of Glasgow and David McIver of Liverpool, the owners of two competing coastal shipping lines between Glasgow and Liverpool, Cunard had, in 1840, founded the British and North American Royal Mail Steam Packet Company (later known as Cunard Steam Ship Company), and had accumulated a starting capital of £270,000, to which he contributed the amount of the Government subsidies he had received. The remaining £215,000 came from businessmen in Glasgow and Manchester. In addition, he had arranged with several Glasgow and Greenock shipbuilders for the construction of four wooden paddle steamers, the *Britannia, Acadia, Columbia and Caledonia,* for which John Napier, the experienced marine engine manufacturer, was contracted to supply the necessary lateral balance engines.

The breath-taking speed with which Cunard confronted his competitors with a *fait accompli* was emphasised by the fact that all four of his ships were ready to sail in 1840. After forty and thirty-three transatlantic round-trips respectively, the *Britannia* and *Acadia* were sold to the North German Confederation Navy in 1849.

The disappointing result of the *President's* maiden voyage, together with the fierce competition from Cunard, caused her owners to take the utterly unexpected and abrupt step of dismissing Captain Fayrer, one day before the ship was to sail for New York. The departure of the steamer under his command had however still been advertised in Gore's *General Advertiser* on 17 September. Captain M M Keane was appointed in Fayrer's place, allowing the *President* to leave for New York on 1 October 1840, as scheduled.

But the subject was far from closed. The friends of the dismissed captain convened a public hearing in the Exchange News and Underwriter's Room, for Wednesday, 30 September at 11 o'clock. It was attended by many influential businessmen from Liverpool, most of the Naval officers resident in the city, and many English and American captains of commercial vessels. The cotton merchant Thomas Todd, principal owner of Todd, Jackson & Co., was elected to chair the meeting. The purpose of it, he said, was to enquire into the cause of the late abrupt dismissal of Captain Fayrer from the command of the *President*. He believed the public had a right to know the reasons for the dismissal, as the prestige of a vessel was dependent mainly on the character of her captain.

Fayrer had served in the Royal Navy with distinction, had been wounded defending his country, and had acquired an impeccable reputation in the merchant marine. He had been entrusted with the *President*, in preference to other applicants, principally for the ability and skill that he had displayed in command of the *Liverpool*.

A passenger, Samuel Cossins, got up and reported that they had been disappointed that the passage lasted sixteen days, but the captain could not be blamed for this. They were convinced that he had done everything possible to make the passage a swift one. An experienced engineer, William Jones, who had also been on board, commented that if the directors wished the *President* to sail faster, she would have to be equipped with stronger engines; a Mr Daniel Neilson had calculated that instead of the available 540 h.p., an additional 270 h.p. at least would be required. Experts, colleagues and passengers were all in support of Captain Fayrer and expressed their disapproval of the company's action. Fayrer was not however reappointed and he once again turned his attention to the development of steam packet services, this time to the West Indies.

The Loss of the SS President

Shortly after Fayrer had been dismissed, the *President* foundered at sea without trace, in 1841. The reasons remain unresolved, but they are certainly mysteriously misrepresented in the oil painting that illustrates the front cover of this book. The picture, from the studio of the landscape painter Andreas Achenbach (1815-1910) of Dusseldorf, is signed and dated 1842. It portrays the *President* striking an iceberg in a Titantic-like disaster. Icebergs were not however as far south as this when the ship was lost, and it is much more probable that the paddle steamer went down in a storm that was raging on 12 March 1841. This is what William J. Leathern portrayed with greater credibility in another oil painting, 'The *President* as last seen signalling with the Brig *Pearl*,' now in the Merseyside Maritime Museum.[24]

The West Indian Steam Packet Service

A sailing ship Packet Service had long been in operation from Falmouth to the West Indies, but the advent of steamships led to the commencement of a new Steam Packet Service from Southampton in 1841. Four new steam driven vessels, the *Forth, Solway, Tweed* and *Clyde*, were assembled to be dispatched to the various stations from which the new company would operate to secure the regularity of mails. Fayrer was chosen to inaugurate the service, in command of the *Forth*, 1939 tons, and sailed for Nassau, Havana, New Orleans, Tampico and Vera Cruz, before returning to Havana to collect the mails for England on 26 January. He was shortly followed by the three other ships, all of them commanded by naval officers.[25]

HMS Tenedos in the Floating Dock, Bermuda

Command of HMS Tenedos, 1843

For the advice he had provided to the Government from his broad experience of steam navigation, Fayrer was given the opportunity to return to the Navy on full pay in 1843, when he was appointed to command *HMS Tenedos*. The ship, lying at Portsmouth, was being converted to a prison ship to transport prisoners from the hulks there to the West Indies. On his arrival at Bermuda, he was instructed to remain there as Agent for the Colonial Service, which he did until 1847, when after being criticised for irregularities in his accounts he took leave of absence and returned to England.[26]

Intentions for a Packet Service to Australasia

On 22 April 1848, a New Zealand paper, the *Nelson Examiner,* reported the contents of a private letter from the Channel Islands, dated 13 December 1847, indicating that prior to his retirement, Fayrer intended to establish a steam packet service to the Antipodes. 'The India and Australia Royal Steam Packet Company via Egypt, has its agent here in Jersey - Lieutenant R J Fayrer, who expects, he tells me, to set it going in the Spring. He goes overland via Suez, and then is to command the steamer going to New South Wales, etc. He has established the American and West Indian steamers, and when he has done the Pacific, retires.' A prospectus for the project was printed, but is seems doubtful that anything very much came of it.[27]

Retirement and Death in France

R J Fayrer retired from the Navy in 1848, with the rank of Commander, and was resident with his wife Agnes at Warnley Lodge, St Saviour, Jersey, in the Channel Islands at the 1851 Census. Later he moved to France, where his wife Agnes died at Dinan in 1863, aged 63 years. Commander Fayrer died on 20 April 1869, aged 81 years.

3

Midshipman Edward Birbeck Fayrer RN

Edward Birbeck Fayrer was the third son of Captain Joseph Fayrer of Milnthorpe, and the younger brother of the Rev Joseph Fayrer and Commander Robert John Fayrer RN. He was born 9 May 1791 and baptized at Heversham Church on 29 June. He entered the Royal Navy in 1805, aged 14 years, three years after his elder brother Robert John Fayrer.

As a midshipman of six years standing, Edward Fayrer, aged 21, was serving in *HMS Defence* when she was wrecked in a storm at the entrance to the Baltic Sea on 23 December 1811, and his death was the occasion for the placing of the family memorial in Heversham Church, by his brother Robert John.

The loss of *HMS Defence* and *HMS St George* in the Christmas gale of 1811 was one of the greatest tragedies the Navy had ever faced. Only 18 men survived out of the two crews numbering in total 1425 officers and ratings.

The Christmas Gale of 1811

For the maintenance of its fleet during the Napoleonic Wars, the Navy relied primarily on stores of flax, hemp and tar from Scandinavia and Russia, and upon the convoys carrying them to Britain through the Baltic and North Sea.

The route was treacherous, the seas were relatively shallow and the waters rough where the North Sea caught incoming waves from the Atlantic, which collided with other wave action originating in the English Channel. The Baltic and its entrance were narrow, with foul weather often preventing accurate position finding. A gale would immediately place a ship in danger of being driven onto a lee shore.

This was never more clearly demonstrated than on Christmas Eve, 1811. A large convoy sailed from Hanö Bay, Sweden on 9 November 1811, bound for England. It consisted of approximately 130 merchantmen escorted by *HMS St George*, *HMS Defence* and *HMS Cressy*, with *St George* flying the flag of Rear Admiral Robert Carthew Reynolds.

HMS Defence

The voyage started going wrong on 15 November when a gale hit the convoy while it was at anchor off Bornholm Island. Some thirty of the merchant ships were driven aground and wrecked. One of them, a large vessel, broke free from its anchors, crossed in front of the *St George* and severed her anchor cable. As remedial action, the captain of the *St George* immediately cut away the other anchors to allow the ship to be maneuvered, but the storm increased in ferocity, driving her towards the shore. The flag captain, David Oliver Guion, wanted to cut away the masts to stop the ship's drift, but Admiral Reynolds, probably concerned about the delay it would cause for his convoy, refused until it was too late. *St George* was driven aground and only refloated with great difficulty, losing her rudder in the process.

When the storm abated, *Cressy* towed *St George* into what was then called Wingo Sound at Gothenburg. *HMS Hero* and *HMS Grasshopper* were already there, and were ordered to escort the convoy home.

A month elapsed while *St George* was refitted and another convoy assembled. On 17 December they again got to sea, with *St George* using jury masts and a type of temporary steering gear called a Pakenham's Rudder.

The new convoy consisted of *St George* and her consorts, accompanied for a time by another convoy escorted by *Victory, Vigo, Dreadnought,* and *Orion.*

On 19 December the full force of another gale hit the convoy. The *Defence* remained close to *St George,* but the *Cressy* was unable to hold her position. The storm abated a little on 22 December when the opinion of those aboard *Cressy* and *Defence* was that *St George* was in worse shape than she appeared.

The storm returned in full force on 23 December, when Captain Pater in *Cressy* was of the opinion that they were very near shore, and if he was to save his vessel he must move her out to sea. No signals were forthcoming from *St George,* so Captain Pater acted independently and gave the necessary orders to save *Cressy.*

The perception aboard *Cressy* and *Defence* was that Admiral

Reynolds did not think it necessary to wear ship and while *Cressy* did so, the captain of *Defence* thought it his duty to remain on station near *St George*. In fact nothing could be farther from the truth. Aboard *St George* they were heroically trying to wear ship, but the violence of the storm shredded sails as soon as they were set.

Shortly after midnight on Christmas Eve 1811, *St George* and *Defence* went aground at Jutland, Denmark. Within three hours both ships were beaten to pieces by the surging waves. Of the 865 officers and men on *St George* only 12 survived, while on *Defence* all but six of the 560 crew members perished.[1]

The tragedy was over, and with it the young life of Edward Birbeck Fayrer. A panageric in the *Lancaster Gazette* on 15 February 1812 lamented that 'To the enterprising spirit of the mariner, he joined the duties of a Christian, and the mild manners of a gentleman', adding the final verse from *The Mariner's Dream* by William Dimond:

> Days, months, years and ages, shall circle away,
> And still the wide waters about thee shall roll-
> Earth loses thy pattern ever and aye,
> O Sailor Boy! Sailor Boy! Peace to thy soul ! [2]

The beach at Thorsminde, Denmark, resting place of Edward Birbeck Fayrer and the crews of HMS Defence and HMS St George

4

Sir Joseph Fayrer, Bt, FRS

West Indian Packet Service Midshipman
Naval Surgeon
Pioneer of Tropical Medicine
Surgeon General of India

Sir Joseph Fayrer, the first baronet, was the second son of Commander Robert John Fayrer RN and his wife Agnes, and the grandson of Captain Joseph Fayrer, Master Mariner, of Harmony Hill, Milnthorpe.

He was born at Plymouth on 6 December 1824, while his father was master of a free trader sailing between England and India. His ship, the *Madras*, sailed from Plymouth, which was more convenient than northern ports for the embarkation of influencial passengers for passage to India.[1]

The Fayrer tenancy of Haverbrack Cottage at Haverbrack, near Milnthorpe, was relinquished in 1822, but close connections with Westmorland were still maintained and residency later resumed.[2]

In his *Recollections of My Life*, Sir Joseph recounts that his earliest memories were of Haverbrack, and whilst there, of making the acquaintance of William Wordsworth, Hartley Coleridge, and his father's friend John Wilson (Christopher North). His family were certainly resident in Ambleside by 1831, where his father was described as a shipowner.[3]

At the age of about eleven, in 1835, the future Sir Joseph and his brother were at a school run by the Rev R Wallace at Dalrymple, Ayrshire. His brother later went to a public school in England, while Joseph returned home to Portpatrick to study under a tutor.[4]

The Fayrers moved to Liverpool in 1840, when Joseph was aged fourteen, and for a time he studied engineering. Visits from his father's British and American friends, many of them engaged in shipping as owners, mariners or passengers, made him again consider the possibility of a seagoing career for himself. One of his father's former Royal Navy friends, Captain Lord John Churchill, *HMS Druid*, had made an offer to take him as a midshipman, which was declined. Later, by the time he was sixteen, he was too old to enter the Navy in the rank of Midshipman.[5]

West India Steam Packet Ship RMS Thames

As a result of his father's involvement with the new West Indian steam-packet service from Southampton, he was nontheless able to make a voyage to the West Indies and South America as a packet service midshipman aboard the

RMS Thames (Captain P. Hast RN). With naval officers in command, packet service ships had a regime like naval vessels, or those of the prestigious East India Company, and their midshipmen wore uniforms. Joseph made three voyages in the mail packet service before giving up the career, seeing in it no prospect of success.[6]

Medical Training

The adoption of a medical career seems to have occurred by chance. On retirement from the West Indian Packet Service in 1843, his father had been appointed commander of *HMS Tenedos*, with instructions to sail her to Bermuda, where he established her as a prison hulk, with himself as superintendent. Joseph accompanied him on the voyage, and after an outbreak of yellow fever occurred while he was in the West Indies, his attention was turned towards medicine.[7]

Returning to England in October 1844, he enrolled at the Charing Cross Hospital, where his fellow students included William Guyer Hunter, born at Calcutta and later Surgeon General in India, and Thomas Henry Huxley, one of the first adherents to Darwin's theory of evolution. At the end of his second year he was appointed house surgeon at the Westminster Ophthalmic Hospital. He was admitted MRCS England in July 1847, and FRCS in 1878.[8]

Nautical connections remained strong however and on 4 August 1847 he received a commission in the Royal Naval Medical Service, on the staff at the Royal Naval Hospital at Haslar, Portsmouth. This commission was resigned soon afterwards, when the opportunity occurred for him to travel with Lord Mount-Edgcumbe on a tour through France, Germany, and Italy.

With the continent destablised by revolutions, 1848 was a tumultuous year to be travelling in Europe and while they were at Palermo, the Sicilian revolution broke out, giving Fayrer his first experience of gunshot wounds.

On arrival at Rome in April, he took the opportunity to study at the university and obtained the degree of Doctor of Medicine (MD) in 1849.[9]

India

After the European tour, Fayrer decided not to continue in the Naval Medical Service, and on 29 June 1850 he left England for Calcutta, to become an assistant surgeon in Bengal. It was the beginning of a connection with the Indian Medical Service that lasted for forty-five years, half of the time being spent in England.

Arriving at Fort William in October 1850, he spent two years at Chinsura, Cherrapunji, in the Khasi Hills. Outstanding service as an assistant surgeon with the Burma field force in the Pegu war of 1852, led Lord Dalhousie to appoint him as the Residency surgeon at Lucknow in July 1853. Later, in September 1854, he received an additional appointment as honorary Assistant Resident, involving political duties, whilst in March 1856 he was also appointed civil surgeon of Lucknow and superintendent of its charitable institutions.[10]

Dr Fayrer married Bethia Mary, eldest daughter of Brigadier-General Andrew Spens, commander of the troops at Lucknow, on 4 October 1855.

The Great Rebellion and the Seige of Lucknow

The impressive house which the Fayrers occupied within the Lucknow Residency became a centre of operations for resistance to the seige of the town that took place with the spread of the Great Rebellion in 1857. Formerly known as the Indian Mutiny, the insurrection was against the rule of the British East India Company.

The rebellion began on 10 May 1857, as a mutiny of sepoys in the Company's army at the town of Meerut, and soon erupted into further outbreaks at Delhi and other towns of central India.

The causes of the Great Rebellion have long been the subject of Indo-British historical debate. The immediate trigger was the introduction of the Enfield rifled musket, which were rumoured to have cartridges greased with pig and cow fat, causing offence to Muslim and Hindu soldiers respectively. More sophisticated interpretations have suggested a range of causes for discontent, including a punitive tax collection system, a succession of British territorial seizures, and the rise of aggressive Christian evangelism.

Remains of Dr Fayrer's House at the Residency, Lucknow.

The rebellion reached Lucknow on 30 May, and the Residency remained under seige until its final relief on 27 November 1857. Accounts of the British defence were provided by several of the residents, including one by Fayrer himself, in his *Recollections of my Life*. His brother was killed during the insurrection.[11]

After Lucknow had been relieved, in March 1858 Fayrer left for England on furlough, where he took the opportunity of obtaining another MD degree at the University of Edinburgh, in March 1859.[12]

When he returned to India at the end of April he became professor of surgery at the medical college at Calcutta, and in January 1867 was elected president of the Asiatic Society of Bengal, which he had joined in January 1861. In that capacity he proposed a scheme for a zoological society and gardens in Calcutta, which was finally carried out in 1875, when the gardens were opened by the Prince of Wales.[13]

In 1869 Fayrer became surgeon in Calcutta to Lord Mayo, the new Viceroy, and on 1 January 1870 accompanied the duke of Edinburgh on his travels through north-west India. His publications in this period were principally surgical, and they included *Clinical Observations in Surgery* (1863) and *Clinical Surgery in India* (1866).[14]

After India

With failing health, Dr Fayrer returned to Britain in 1872. That year, in spite of his surgical background, he was elected FRCP London, which meant he could not practise surgery in London. Instead, with Thomas Lauder Brunton he resumed research on snake venoms, publishing his most ambitious work, *The Thanatophidia of India* (1872).[15]

Subsequently Fayrer joined the Medical Board of the

India Office in February 1873 and became its President on 8 December, continuing there until January 1895, when he retired from the active list of the Indian army as Surgeon General, with a good pension.[16]

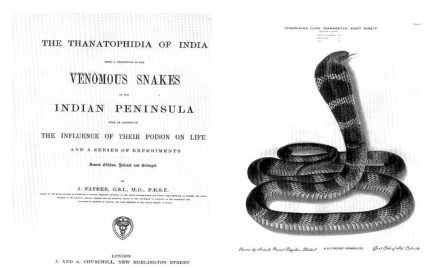

Title Page and Illustration from The Thanatophidia of India

Meanwhile, in 1875, he was selected as a 'spy' for the Queen, to accompany the Prince of Wales on a tour of India. On their return he became honorary physician to the prince, with whom he later formed a lifelong friendship.[17]

Recognition of his scientific research came when Dr Fayrer was elected Fellow of the Royal Society (FRS) in April 1877. Honorary doctorates followed: from Edinburgh in 1878, when on his way he visited Haverbrack, and from St Andrews in 1890.[18] The latter part of his professional life was devoted to lecturing and publishing. As president of the Epidemiological Society he gave an address entitled 'The progress of epidemiology in India' in 1879; and to the Medical Society of London, the Lettsomian lecture on

'Tropical Diseases', in 1881. 'Climate and some of the fevers of India' was the subject of his Croonian lectures at the Royal College of Physicians in 1882.[19]

His standing in Britain and India, coupled with his extraordinary ability as a linguist, made him an ideal choice to represent the government of India at the Intercolonial Congress at Amsterdam, and at the International Sanitary congress held at Rome in May and June 1885. And for the tercentenary of Galileo at Padua in December 1892, he delivered his speech in Italian, representing both the Royal College of Physicians and the University of Edinburgh.[20]

A prolific writer on Indian climatology, the pathology of Indian diseases, sanitation, and above all on venomous snakes, Fayrer's *Thanatophidia* remains the classic contribution to the literature of snakes and snakebites. Printed by the Indian government, it was handsomely illustrated with coloured plates by local members of the Calcutta School of Art.

The clinical outcome of his research was the permanganate treatment of venomous snakebites, but his main conclusions were that there then existed no absolute antidote, and that safety was to be attained only when the bite was in such a position as to make the application of a ligature between it and the heart possible, together with the use of cautery. Later, these opinions were somewhat modified after experiments by Fayrer, Sir Lauder Brunton and Major Leonard Rogers demonstrated that recovery might be expected if a ligature were applied within half a minute or an even a longer period after a bite, the site of the injury being then incised and solid permanganate of potassium rubbed in.[21]

Eminent Doctors
Illustrated London News 1894
Dr Fayrer is second from the Right on the back row

The Baronetcy

The ultimate accolade came on 7 February 1896 when Doctor Fayrer was invested as knight baronet and styled Sir Joseph Fayrer, Bt, of Devonshire Street, St Marylebone, London.[22]

The remainder of his life was passed chiefly at Falmouth, where, always actively interested in sports, he indulged his passions for deep-sea fishing and yachting.[23]

He died at his home, Belfield, Wood Lane, Falmouth, on 21 May 1907. His wife, Bethia Mary, died in 1916. Their eldest son, Robert Andrew, born on 27 June 1856, had died on 28 December 1904 and he was succeeded as second baronet by his eldest surviving son, Joseph, who joined the Royal Army Medical Corps.[24]

A grant of arms was made to the second baronet: Argent on a bend invected Sable between a chief an eastern crown Gules and in base the staff of Aesculapius Proper enfiled with a like crown three horseshoes Or. The arms are surmounted by a crest: In front of a sword erect Proper pommel, and hilt Or, a horseshoe Or, between two wings Gules. The family motto is *Ne tentes aut perfice* (Do not Try, but Succeed).[25]

Throughout their subsequent involvement with India, the family was increasingly connected with the Army medical service, but nautical traditions did not entirely cease. After Sandhurst and service as a Lieutenant with the King's Own Borderers during WWI, the third baronet, Sir Joseph Herbert Spens Fayrer DSC, son of the second baronet and Ella, daughter of Colonel W A J Mayhew, Bengal Army, was at sea whaling in the South Atlantic with Christian Salvesen. On the outbreak of WWII, he was commissioned as Lt Commander in the RNVR, commanding the trawlers *HMS Acacia* and *HMS Herschell*, and the corvettes *HMS Stonecrop* and *HMS Balsam*, escorts for Channel and Arctic convoys. He was awarded the DSC on 21 March 1941.[26]

Flower Class Corvette HMS Balsam

His son, Sir John Lang Macpherson Fayrer, the 4th baronet, by his second wife, Helen Diane Scott, resides in Edinburgh, and is the author of *Child Development from Birth to Adolescence* (Moray House, 1992).[27]

The family's connections with Westmorland, through at least three generations, have now virtually come to an end, but the maritime influences of the former minor seaport of Milnthorpe have run deep in the exploits and achievements of this remarkable but largely forgotten local seafaring dynasty, of which Harmony Hall, Milnthorpe, and the memorial in Heversham Church are now the most prominent South Lakeland vestiges.

Notes

Chapter 1: Captain Joseph Fayrer

1 thepeerage.com
2 Date on Memorial at Heversham Church
3 School archive at CRO(Kendal), but apparently no 18th Century admissions lists have survived.
4 St George's Quay Tonnage Book, Lancaster MM
5 William R. O'Byrne, *Naval Biographical Dictionary* (London, 1849) p.349
6 Jamaica Merchant Shipping at Jamaica: http://jamaicanfamilysearch.com/Samples2/ships1776.htm
7 thepeerage.com
8 Adams's *Weekly Courant* (Chester), 16 February 1779
9 *General Evening Post*, 20 May 1779
10 *St. James's Chronicle* (London) of 9 June 1781; Liverpool Maritime Museum M D/EARLE/1/7
11 Ibid.
12 Ibid.
13 *English Chronicle* (London), 22 October 1789
14 *Minutes of the Evidence taken at the bar of the House of Lords, on the order made for taking into consideration the present trade to Africa…*(London, 1792)
15 Archibald Dalzel, *The History of Dahomy* (London, 1793)

16 Haggerty, Sheryllynne and John, 'Visual Analytics of an Eighteenth-Century Network' in *Enterprise and Society*, 11(1), 1-25. 2010

17 Ibid.

18 *Woodfall's Register* (London), 3 August 1793

19 *Evening Mail* (London), 14 October 1793

20 Nikolaus Pevsner, *The Buildings of England Cumberland and Westmorland* (Penguin, 1967) p.277

21 Sir Joseph Fayrer, *Recollections...*(William.Blackwood and Sons, London and Edinburgh, 1900)

22 Kendal to Liverpool stage coach service began in 1763, but see Leonard Smith, *Westmorland Dialogues* (Lensden Publishing, 2011) p.12, for how the sea route was still being taken in 1792.

23 Alice Palmer, *The Low Wood Gunpowder Company Its Inception and Early Growth 1798-1808* (Gunpowder Mills Study Group, London, 1998)

24 Lancashire County Record Office, DDLO DDLO/Box 2 Bundle 5

25 Ibid.

26 Death recorded on Memorial

27 Abstract of Will, National Archives CO 37/117; Act of Parliament 59 Geo. 3. c. 46. (Printed), CRO(K) WD AG/Box 105

Chapter 2: Commander Robert John Fayrer RN

1 Heversham Church Registers, CRO(K) WPR8/1/1

2 *Dictionary of National Biography*

3 Joseph Allen, *The New Navy List and General Record of Services of Officers in the Royal Navy and Royal Marine* (London, 1847) p.123

4 William R.O'Byrne, *Naval Biographical Dictionary* (London, 1849), p.349

5 Florence Marryat (Mrs Rose Church) *Life and Letters of Captain Marryat*, pp. 24-28

6 Many books available, but see online, Thomas Cochrane, *Autobiography of a Seaman* (Maclaren and Company) http://www.archive.org/details/autobiogra phyofs00dunduoft and *The Life of Thomas Cochrane*, http://www.gutenberg.org/ebooks/13351

7 O'Byrne, op cit.

8 Beetham Church Register

9 *Liverpool Mercury*, 21 June 1816

10 *Lancaster Gazette and General Advertiser*, 28 July 1821

11 Ibid., 12 October 1822

12 *Morning Post*, 7 March 1825

13 *Hampshire Telegraph and Sussex Chronicle*, 11 June, 1827

14 Lancelot Shadwell, *Reports of Cases decided in the High Court of Chancery*, Vol IX, p.300

15 *House of Commons Papers*, Vol. 28 pp.203, 216-219

16 *Athenaeum: Journal of Literature, Science and Fine Arts*, 6 July 1850

17 *Belfast News-Letter*, 28 February 1834

18 *Hampshire Telegraph and Sussex Chronicle*, 25 October 1830

19 *Proceedings of the Zoological Society of London*, 27 February 1844

20 *Morning Chronicle* (London), 12 September, 1838

21 *Athenaeum: Journal of Literature, Science and Fine Arts*, 11 May 1850

22 *The Standard* (London), 22 December 1838

23 *Liverpool Mercury,* 25 December 1840

24 Lars U. Scholl, 'The Loss of the Steamship President: A painting by the German artist Andreas Achenbach', *Northern Mariner/Le marin du nord,* XV No. 3, (July 2005), pp.53 -71.

25 *Hampshire Telegraph and Sussex Chronicle,* 15 May 1843; *Hampshire Advertiser and Salisbury Guardian,* 18 December 1843

26 National Archives, CO 37/117 - CO 37/124

27 The Baring Archive No. 2.343 1847: *The India and Australia Royal Mail Steam Packet Co. Prospectus, via Egypt.* Printed

Chapter 3: Midshipman Edward Birbeck Fayrer RN

1 http://ageofsail.wordpress.com

2 *Lancaster Gazette,* 15 February 1812

Chapter 4: Sir Joseph Fayrer, Bt FRS

1 Sir Joseph Fayrer, *Recollections of my life* (William Blackford and Sons, 1900)

2 *Lancaster Gazette,* 12 October 1822

3 *Recollections,* p.2

4 Ibid. p.4

5 Ibid. pp.5,6

6 Ibid. p.7

7 Ibid. p.13

8 Ibid. pp.14, 21, 22

9 Ibid. pp. 24-35

10 Ibid. pp.48 -83

11 Ibid. pp. 130-218

12 Ibid. p.246

13 Ibid. p.259

14 *British Medical Journal*, 25 May 1907, p.1281

15 Ibid. p. 326

16 Ibid. p.1280

17 Ibid. p.1280

18 *Recollections...*, p.430

19 *Dictionary of National Biography*

20 *Recollections*, p.489

21 *Dictionary of National Biography*

22 Ibid.

23 *British Medical Journal*, 25 May 1907, p.1280

24 Ibid.

25 R. S. Boumphrey, Christopher Roy Hudleston and Joseph Hughes, *An armorial for Westmorland and Lonsdale*(Cumberland and Westmorland Antiquarian and Archaeological Society, 1975), p.113

26 http://www.unithistories.com/officers/RNVR_offi cersF.html; http://www.uboat.net/allies/command ers/commanders.php?cID=882; *London Gazette* 1941

27 J. Fayrer, *Child Development from Birth to Adolescence* (Moray House, 1992)

Index